1/16

# SASHA SINGS

## UNDERSTANDING PARTS OF A SENTENCE

by Cari Meister

illustrated by Ben Whitehouse

PICTURE WINDOW BOOKS
a capstone imprint

Sasha sings.

Sasha sings loudly.

Sasha sings softly.

6

Sasha sings loudly and softly.

Shimmering Sasha sings
loudly and softly.

8

Shimmering Sasha sings loudly and softly for her fans.

Shimmering Sasha sings loudly and softly for her fans, but not today.

The doctor comes.

"Your throat must rest. Your throat must rest for two weeks," he says.

"Cheer up," says the director. "You
cannot sing, but you can still dance."

Sasha dances.

Sasha dances fast.

Sasha dances joyfully.

Sasha dances fast and joyfully.

Spangled Sasha dances
fast and joyfully.

Spangled Sasha dances
fast and joyfully through
the theater.

Someday, shimmering Sasha will
sing loudly and softly for her fans.

But for now, spangled Sasha dances fast
and joyfully through the theater.

BRAVO, SASHA!

# About Parts of a Sentence

A sentence is a group of words that make a complete thought. All sentences need two things: a subject and a predicate. The subject tells who or what. The predicate tells what the subject does or is. Step by step, building a sentence looks like this:

**STEP 1** Pick a subject. A subject is a noun. A noun is a word for a person, place, or thing.

Archie
The spaceship

**STEP 2** Add a predicate (what a subject does or is). A predicate always has a verb. A verb is either an action or a "being" word.

Archie **slept.**
The spaceship **zooms.**

After this step, you can stop, if you want. You now have a complete thought. You have a sentence!

**STEP 3** To make a more interesting sentence, add an adjective. An adjective gives information about a noun. It describes the noun.

**Tired** Archie slept.
The **silver** spaceship zooms.

**STEP 4** You can also give information about a verb by adding an adverb. See how "adverb" has the word "verb" in it? (Hint: Many adverbs end in -ly.)

Tired Archie slept **soundly.**
The silver spaceship zooms **fast.**

**STEP 5** Want to add more? Prepositions show the relationship between nouns or pronouns. Conjunctions link two parts of a sentence together.

Tired Archie slept soundly **through** the morning. (preposition)

The silver spaceship zooms fast, **but** the blue spaceship zooms faster. (conjunction)

*This book ends. This silly hippo book ends. This silly hippo book ends, but smart readers will quickly flip to the beginning and read it again!*

# Read More

**Dahl, Michael.** *If You Were a Noun, a Verb, an Adjective, an Adverb, a Pronoun, a Conjunction, an Interjection, a Preposition.* Word Fun. Minneapolis: Picture Window Books, 2009.

**Rosenthal, Amy Krouse.** *Exclamation Mark.* New York: Scholastic Press, 2013.

**Walton, Rick.** *Around the House the Fox Chased the Mouse: An Adventure in Prepositions.* Layton, Utah: Gibbs Smith, 2011.

# Internet Sites

FactHound offers a safe, fun way to find Internet sites related to this book. All of the sites on FactHound have been researched by our staff.

Here's all you do:

Visit *www.facthound.com*

Type in this code: 9781479569649

Super-cool stuff! Check out projects, games and lots more at **www.capstonekids.com**

# Look for all the books in the series:

**The BIG Problem (and the Squirrel Who Eventually Solved It)**
Understanding Adjectives and Adverbs

**The Duckster Ducklings Go to Mars**
Understanding Capitalization

**Frog. Frog? Frog!**
Understanding Sentence Types

**Monsters Can Mosey**
Understanding Shades of Meaning

**Sasha Sings**
Understanding Parts of a Sentence

**They're Up to Something in There**
Understanding There, Their, and They're

**whatever says mark**
Knowing and Using Punctuation

**When and Why Did the Horse Fly?**
Knowing and Using Question Words

Special thanks to our adviser, Terry Flaherty, PhD, Professor of English, Minnesota State University, Mankato, for his expertise.

Editor: Jill Kalz
Designer: Ted Williams
Creative Director: Nathan Gassman
Production Specialist: Katy LaVigne
The illustrations in this book were created digitally.

Picture Window Books are published by Capstone,
1710 Roe Crest Drive, North Mankato, Minnesota 56003
www.capstonepub.com

Library of Congress Cataloging-in-Publication Data
Meister, Cari, author.
  Sasha sings : understanding parts of a sentence / by Cari Meister.
    pages cm.—(Picture window books. Language on the Loose.)
  Includes bibliographical references and index.
  Summary: "Introduces basic parts of a sentence—including subjects, predicates, and modifiers—through the telling of an original story"—Provided by publisher.
  ISBN 978-1-4795-6964-9 (library binding)
  ISBN 978-1-4795-6968-7 (paperback)
  ISBN 978-1-4795-6972-4 (eBook PDF)
1. English language—Sentences—Juvenile literature. 2. English language—Composition and exercises—Juvenile literature. 3. English language—Sentences—Study and teaching (Elementary)
I. Title. II. Title: Understanding parts of a sentence.
PE1441.M45 2016
425—dc23                                            2014049205

Printed in the United States of America in North Mankato, Minnesota.    042015    008823CGF15